Don't Be

A DOUCHEBAG

ONLINE DATING ADVICE I WISH MEN WOULD TAKE

CASSIE LEIGH

TITLES BY CASSIE LEIGH

DATING FOR MEN

Online Dating for Men: The Basics
Don't Be A Douchebag
You Have a Date, Don't F It Up

Also available in The How To Meet A Woman Collection

COOKING-RELATED

Quick & Easy Cooking For One

DATING FOR WOMEN

Online Dating for Women: The Basics
Online Dating Is Hell

DOG-RELATED

Puppy Parenting Basics
Puppy Parenting In An Apartment
Dog Park Basics

CONTENTS

CONTENTS (CONT.)

INTRODUCTION

Here's the deal. Online dating sucks. Half the time, the wrong people are talking to each other and it ends up turning into a real slog. You like someone, they shut you down, and you don't know why.

It can be frustrating. And hard. And time consuming.

This book is meant to help you avoid some of the common pitfalls of online dating from a woman who has been there, done that.

There are a few chapters in here for the legitimate douchebags (which I define as men who want some woman any woman to sleep with or who are so emotionally damaged that they can't handle a real relationship), because if those guys could target their efforts, it'd make the whole experience better for all of us.

So, if you do just want some fun sexy times, stick to the first few chapters. If not, if you really want to find a woman for a lasting relationship, then this book can help. It'll get you past the worst offenses men commit.

Cassie Leigh

I'm not a kind and gentle soul, but if you listen to what I have to say, you'll do better, I promise.

So, with that said, let's get started.

SETTING THE STAGE

First, you need to understand what online dating is like for a reasonably attractive woman.

Let's assume that we're not on one of those sites that structure your communications. It's just a free-for-all, contact-anyone-you-want-say-anything-you-want, situation.

Maybe this woman created a profile last night because she thought it would be fun to see what her personality type is.

(I made that mistake once.)

Or maybe she finally decided that joining that gym wasn't going to result in any romantic possibilities and it was time to give online dating a chance.

Whatever the reason, she creates a profile, puts up a picture that her guy friends like, fills in answers to all the questions (even the stupid ones), and goes to sleep.

She isn't looking for a casual hookup. She wants a relationship. And she says so right there in her profile.

This is what she finds when she wakes up:

You have 22 new messages from The Best Dating Site in the World!

At first, she's excited.

Twenty-two messages! Wow. That's great.

She thought she'd get one or two messages, but twenty-two? There's bound to be someone interesting in there.

She opens the first one.

It's from a guy who explains that he's married and staying in the relationship for the kids, but that he really needs to get some lovin' so he's joined this site looking for someone to sleep with on the side. He saw her profile and found her very attractive.

He, of course, doesn't have a picture on his profile because he doesn't want anyone to know that he's a cheating bastard (my words, not his), but he'd be happy to send a picture along if she's interested.

Right, because obviously she is so desperate to find someone that she'll agree to screwing around with a married man. No.

Delete.

She opens the second one.

It says, "Hey hottie! Whatcha up to tonight?"

She looks and can see that it was sent about a minute after she uploaded her profile picture.

Great to see he couldn't take the time to look at anything other than her photo. Delete.

E-mail three is an obvious cut and paste about the guy. "My name is John and I am thirty-two. I like long walks and am looking for a woman to walk with me through life."

Couldn't even take the time to find just one little thing they might have in common and add it to his obvious form message?

Delete.

E-mails four through ten are a variation on e-mails two and three.

Delete. Delete. Delete…

E-mail eleven is another with no profile picture from a guy asking her if she's into younger men.

Delete.

E-mail twelve is from a man about twenty years older than her who says he's looking for someone to have great sex with. His profile picture shows him with a deep tan and a very large boat.

He seems to think this makes him unique or special because he can be upfront about what he's looking for.

Ha! Right. 'Cause no other guy on the site is looking for sex. They just want someone to hold hands with.

Delete.

E-mail thirteen is a long e-mail from a man explaining how much he likes to please women and is looking for someone who will take a firm hand with him.

Ew. Delete.

While reading the first batch of e-mails she's seeing out of the corner of her eye that more men are checking out her profile.

By the time she finishes e-mail fourteen, she has five new messages—all of the "Hey sexy-what's up?" variety.

Delete. Delete. Delete…

If she's new to this, she may actually try to respond to some of these guys.

Nothing wrong with a guy who thinks you're attractive and shoots off a quick e-mail, right?

Wrong.

She'll learn.

Because if she does write back and try to say anything

about what's in her profile—"Sorry, I didn't respond last night. I had to go to salsa classes"—she'll either get no response because the guy was just looking for someone to hook up with right then or she'll get a response that shows that the guy still hasn't read her profile—"So, you do salsa, huh? Cool. Whatcha up to?"

So, here we are. She's read and deleted twenty messages so far.

And now she opens yours.

She's not at her best right now.

She's wondering why she bothers.

She's starting to think she should've just hooked up with that obnoxious frat guy in college who cornered her at that party.

She's thinking that at least if you date a co-worker you know that he can act normal five days out of seven.

She's on the edge.

If you're going to get through to her, you need to be a refreshing ray of sunlight in the dark hell in which she's found herself.

The rest of this book will discuss how you do that. But first we need to cover the douchebags.

(If you want to skip past the chapters for the douchebags, which might be entertaining, but not of much use in terms of advice, go to Chapter 4: So You Really Want to Find Someone.)

SO YOU ARE A DOUCHEBAG

Nothing wrong with that. It takes all types.

What do I mean by this? Well, you're the type of guy who sees women as interchangeable and only good for one thing—satisfying your ego or fucking.

You don't want to get to know someone.

You don't want to form a connection.

You just want to get your rocks off.

That's cool. Why you're reading this book is beyond me, but, whatever. Your money, not mine.

Maybe you'd like to be that kind of guy—the guy who can go online and find someone for the weekend— but you just don't know how to make that happen.

Okay. Let's walk through how this works.

First, the rest of this book is not for you. Because getting laid (if that's all you want) is just a numbers game.

If a woman wants to have sex, what you say isn't all that relevant.

(Try not to be a dumbass and say really offensive things, but, other than that, it doesn't matter much.)

Do you need brilliant pick-up lines?

("Is your father a thief? Did he steal the stars and put them in your eyes?" Okay, so maybe that's not a brilliant one. But use it on a woman when she wants to like you and she'll laugh and you'll think it is.)

No. Brilliance is not required.

This is about sex, not compatibility.

All you need to do is keep going until you find someone who says, "yes."

Don't waste time building up to the question and go back and forth with some woman for a week or two.

(You probably shouldn't ask it in the first message, though. I suspect that might get you banned from some sites.)

So, a few back and forths, a "Hey, wanta hang out?" sent at two in the morning, and move on to the next until one says, "Sure, why not?"

This is where all the "Hey, hottie" messages come from. Guys who don't give a shit who they're talking to.

(If you do give a shit, now you know why that approach doesn't work for guys like you—because it makes you look like one of the douchebags.)

So, like I said, it's a numbers game. Send enough messages to enough women, you will find one to sleep with.

And, great for both of you. I have no problem with people looking for sex who find other people looking for sex.

I just wish they'd leave me out of it.

And how do you leave someone like me out of it?

By taking *ten seconds* to look at the profile of the woman you're about to message.

(Trust me, it'll be worth it. You'll up your hit percentage.)

What do you look for?

Boobs. Fish lips. Obvious selfies. A girl who posts pictures of herself at the bar with ten of her besties or surrounded by tons of guys.

(If the guys are shirtless or sleeveless, add a few extra bonus points.)

Scan the woman's profile.

Lots of text? Not your girl.

Your girl doesn't need to say much more than that she's "fun", "likes to party", and "wants to have a good time."

If she can't spell, even better.

A note here: There will be other women who want to just find someone for sex. Professional types that aren't going to post boob and selfie photos.

Chances are those women will be a little more discreet and focused in what they do, because the last thing they need is a boss or co-worker to see their profile and think the wrong thing.

You may just need to let those women come to you.

What we're talking about here are the low-hanging fruit.

So, to sum up: You want a chick showing off her boobs, making a kissy face at the camera, talking about how much fun she is.

And if there's a picture of her doing shots? Bonus.

Now, some of you are a very special kind of douchebag—you're married or otherwise in a committed relationship and looking for something on the side.

Guess what? You get your very own chapter. Lucky you!

SO YOU'RE MARRIED

Fuck you. Leave me alone.

Okay, now that we've gotten past that. Let's chat.

You're married or you've been living with a woman for years. And it isn't enough for you.

The love is gone. She no longer wants to have sex. You're tired of all of your lovey dovey time involving *Playboy* magazine and your own hand.

Got it.

I'm sorry that life sucks so bad for you.

But why are you contacting this woman?

Did you see the part in her profile where she said she wanted a relationship? And, no, screwing you twice a week when it's convenient and you can get away with it is not what she meant.

There are women who like screwing married men.

There are women who like screwing any and all men. (See previous chapter.)

Find one of them.

Oh, but you're *special*. You need to have a *connection* with a woman and those brainless party girls just aren't enough for you.

You want a woman with substance—an intelligent, funny, witty woman who can have a scintillating conversation *and* orgasmic sex.

Here's your problem: She's intelligent, funny, witty, and looking for a real relationship.

Do you really think she wants to get involved with you? No. No, she does not.

Now, some women who meet all of the above criteria do make stupid choices. But they generally don't do so online with some stranger they've never met.

They get a little too close to that co-worker when they're working on that high-stress, all-hours project. Or they find themselves drawn to that funny and charming guy on their kickball team.

They do not, as a general rule, respond to married douchebags trolling for women on dating sites.

If you can't just settle for one of the women who would happily screw you and instead have to go for one of the women who really, really does not want to get involved with a guy like you, then you need to develop that in the real world, not online.

You could lie. You could pretend to be single until she's so far under your spell that she goes against her better instincts, but you're playing with fire.

Because if you've misjudged, this is the type of woman who will burn you hard when she finds out.

Call your wife, hard. Call your boss, hard.

Grab you by the balls and twist, hard.

Don't do it. It's not worth it.

What you need to do is find a woman who is expressly looking for a douche like you.

How do you do this?

Well, I'm not going to name any sites here, but there are sites out there that will let you find a woman like this.

First, there are the obvious ones that are specifically geared toward committed types like you.

(If you don't know which ones I'm talking about, I wonder if you ever watch the news or have any friends.)

Second, there's also at least one mainstream site that has questions designed to let you find those types of women. (And it's free, too!)

This is what you do. You go to that free site and you find the questions that say, "I want to screw around with a guy who's already in a relationship" and you tell the site that you want women who answered that question "YES, PLEASE! SOUNDS AWESOME."

You make that of utmost importance for your match results. And, for every possible match, you see how the woman you're about to approach answered that question *before* you reach out to her.

You don't waste your time messaging women who answered, "HELL NO. THAT GUY WOULD BE A SCUM BUCKET THAT I WOULDN'T TOUCH WITH A TEN-FOOT POLE."

Got it? Pretty simple.

There are women out there who want this kind of thing. Please find them and leave the rest of us alone.

(Oh, and if you're not just looking for sex with anyone living and of the opposite sex who meets your general physical requirements, have you stopped to think that maybe, just maybe it isn't sex that's lacking in your relationship? Maybe instead of looking for some strange online you should put some effort into your relationship and fix your shit instead? Or, dare I say it, move on?)

(Maybe your wife no longer wants to sleep with you because you've become a passive-aggressive asshole or a distant, entitled jerk. Just a thought.)

(And, no, I don't feel bad for insulting you. You made a commitment to someone and you are now lying and cheating and deceiving them. I have no sympathy for you. I wouldn't even play the world's smallest violin for you. Fix your shit.)

If you have permission from your significant other, that's a different story.

I still don't want to get involved with you, but I don't think you're pond scum. You're just fishing off the wrong pier.

Join a polyamory group or look for women open to that kind of thing. Just leave those of us who want committed monogamous one-to-one relationships out of it, okay?

SO YOU REALLY WANT TO FIND SOMEONE

Good. We've got some work to do, but, hopefully, by the end of this book you'll have a lot better idea of what triggers a woman to delete your messages.

Keep in mind, though, that this is just one woman's perspective. Other women may feel differently about some of these issues.

What's key (and it'll come up repeatedly throughout the rest of this book) is that you listen to the woman you are approaching. Look at her pictures, her user name, what she says in her profile, and her e-mails to you.

Listen.

And remember that this is from the viewpoint of the woman who barely convinced herself to try this whole online dating thing.

She's living her life happily enough but wouldn't mind finding someone to share it with.

She's not going to take a lot of shit. She's not going to give a guy a chance just because "you never know."

This is a woman who can get by just fine. She pays her own bills and has an education and career.

She doesn't need to be saved.

She isn't desperately lonely.

She gets enough male attention in the real world, so she isn't on there to get her ego stroked.

She'd just kinda, sorta like to find someone she can click with.

So, how do you present yourself as the guy she's looking for?

Well, let's start at the beginning.

STEP ONE —
IS SHE A GOOD FIT FOR YOU?

First things first, you need to decide whether this woman is a good fit for *you*.

Of course she is. Look at that smile. Isn't she pretty?

She looks like a nice person, doesn't she?

The type who'd sit across the table from you and listen sympathetically while you talk about what a tough day you had at work.

STOP.

Stop right there.

Let's figure out what it is that you actually want.

Do you like women who cuss? No? *Have you looked at her profile?*

I can't count all that high, but it seems to me that there's a lot of damn and shit being used there. Do you imagine that this woman's not going to cuss in person when she does in her profile?

Do you like women who are active? Yes? Okay, *have you looked at her profile?*

What's that say under hobbies? Reading, board games, and Tetris. Is that an active woman?

Or, on the flip side, when was the last time you went for a hike? Three years ago?

Nothing wrong with that, but what are you doing imagining that the woman who lists her hobbies as rock climbing and marathon running is going to be a good match?

Maybe you do share a ton of interests. Great.

Is she nice?

Look, my profile reads a lot like this book. I'm snarky and obnoxious and fairly hostile. And yet I get men who are clearly accommodating and sweet writing me all the time. Why??

I'm not a mean person. I don't like to hurt people. But dealing with a sweet guy like that makes me feel as bad as kicking a puppy.

I've never kicked a puppy, by the way. But I have certainly had to shut down a perfectly nice, innocuous guy because he was clearly not going to be able to deal with me as I am.

If you're a nice guy and you aren't looking for a nice girl, you need to reconsider what you're doing.

It's not that nice guys finish last. It's that nice guys are just like any other guy and they focus far too much on physical appearance and far too little on compatibility, so end up chasing the wrong women.

Stop doing that.

Find someone who shares your interests.

Someone with a similar outlook and perspective.

A woman with the same values as you.

You're not going to listen to me, but I'm telling you:
Ignore the picture.

Don't Be A Douchebag

Not forever!
Just long enough to see if she's compatible.
This is the approach you should take:
Compatible? Yes. Attractive? Yes. Okay, reach out.
What most men do:
Attractive? Yes. Reach out.
Don't do that to yourself. The information is there, use it.

STEP TWO —
BE WHO YOU ARE

In my last foray into online dating I saw at least two profiles where the guys were over forty but listed their ages as thirty-nine because they didn't want to get left out of searches.

Bullshit. Those guys were insecure. They turned forty and it freaked them out, so they thought the best approach was to lie about it.

You know what that tells me about them? That they're liars.

And guys who lie are douchebags.

There is no "turning forty" exception. A lie is a lie.

What else is that guy going to lie about?

So he was a little paranoid that turning forty meant women in their thirties wouldn't want him anymore.

(Wrong, by the way. And even more wrong when it comes to certain women in their twenties.)

It was a little lie, he admitted it in his profile. No big deal, right?

Wrong.

Here's the deal. We're talking about people looking for a relationship here. This should be built upon openness and trust.

If some guy thinks it's no big deal to lie about his age, what else will he lie about?

What happens when he loses his job?

Is he one of those guys that will pretend to still have a job, dress up in his suit every morning, and go sit at Starbucks all day rather than tell his partner that he's unemployed?

That's not what a woman wants. She hasn't even met this guy yet and he's already broken her trust.

BE WHO YOU ARE.

Own it. List your real hobbies. List your real profession.

Do not say you're a lawyer, when you're just an assistant to one. (True example, by the way.)

Do not say you draw comics when you drew one comic two years ago. (Another true example.)

A woman who is looking for a real relationship is going to pay attention to what you say. And she'll believe it, too.

If you lie to this woman, she'll walk away.

This myth that you can make a woman fall in love with you and then tell her the truth is a bunch of crap. That is one shaky foundation to build a relationship on.

I'm not saying all women will judge you for a lie or walk away the first time they catch you out.

They should.

Unfortunately, there are lots of forgiving types out there who will probably let it slide.

But is that what you want? To live a lie? To be insecure all the time with the one person who should have your back?

Fake it for the rest of the world, but don't fake it for your partner.

It will collapse at some point and it won't be pretty.

So, own who you are.

Even if it is someone over forty who weighs fifty pounds more than they did ten years ago.

STEP THREE —
CHOOSE THE RIGHT PICTURE

So, you've found someone you like and you want to message her. Good.

First, let's talk about your pictures.

It's tempting, I know it is, to post that picture of you from ten years ago where you looked really frickin' hot.

But that's not who you are now. That's who you were on one day ten years ago.

Let it go.

Be yourself.

Post a current photo. You're not twenty-two anymore. You no longer run around with a killer tan and board shorts all summer.

As a matter of fact, the last time you wore board shorts was in that photo. So, stop it.

Show who you are NOW.

So what if that's a mid-thirties, office-bound, computer nerd?

Own it.

You aren't going to be on the cover of GQ anytime soon. And? So? Does that matter? No.

Are you charming? Can you make a woman laugh? *That* matters.

Your looks are just part of the equation. And they are what they are.

Unless you were planning on getting plastic surgery or inventing a time machine before that first date?

No? Well then…

Post an accurate photo!

Fact of the matter is that confidence will do far more for you than all the plastic surgery in the world.

Now, step back and look at that photo.

Does it reflect who you are?

Does it show what your interests are? What you value?

Too often men feel this need to post photos of themselves looking fun or athletic. So they post that one photo of that one party they went to a year ago even though they're much more the quiet dinner at home type.

(I can't count the number of tuxedo photos I've seen that were from some wedding the guy attended.)

Or they put up a photo of that one tandem skydive they did five years ago that they only did because their best friend threatened to publish certain photos from college if they didn't agree to it.

If it's not representative of you, don't use it.

Don't get me wrong. If you do adventurous things with your life and want to post pictures that show that and some are one-offs, that's fine.

But if you've done two adventurous things in your entire life and those are the pictures you choose to post, you're just creating a false impression of yourself that you now have to live up to.

Another true story: I had some guy reach out to me who it turns out was a fairly successful and interesting entrepreneur.

His profile picture (and user name) made him look like a street punk. Baseball cap tilted to the side, baggy clothes. I think he was even throwing a "hang tough" sign.

The guy in that photo was of no interest to me.

And this guy wasn't even like that anymore. But that's what he was showing to prospective partners, which probably wasn't helping him much.

Oh, and, no matter how bad you look, post a photo.

If you have something seriously wrong with you, I know that's tough to do. It probably means lots of rejection, because many women will judge you based on that photo.

But if it's something that will drive women away from even responding to you, you're probably better off meeting someone in real life and not even trying online dating.

(I know. Scary thought. But letting someone get to know you in real life really can overcome an amazing number of flaws and quirks that people will reject you for online.)

Once again: this idea that you can get a woman to fall in love with you and then reveal the "real you" is BULLSHIT. Especially if you think it can happen online without any in-person contact.

I'm sure it sucks to not be traditionally attractive. But all you have to do is go to the grocery store some weekend and look around at all the couples. There really is someone for everyone.

Can you get a Victoria's Secret model? Well, are you a billionaire with a great sense of humor? Or Jason Statham? No? Then, probably not.

But you can find *someone*. And it'll be a hell of a lot easier to find that person if you're up front with what you look like and who you are *now*.

STEP FOUR —
CHECK YOUR PROFILE

Before you actually message this woman, let's take a quick peek at your profile.

"My friends say I'm a bit of a loner. Lol."

What is that shit?

Did you really *laugh out loud* when you wrote that? No. You did not.

(If you did, may I suggest some counseling?)

Look. Men use "lol" *all the frickin' time*. And *always* in ways like I cited above.

(Yes, that's hyperbole. Deal with it.)

Using "lol" like that makes a man look like a nervous serial killer.

Don't do it.

Go through your profile and eliminate every single "lol."

Every. Single. One.

You don't want to? Fine. Just know that you will not get started with a woman like me if you leave them in.

I see "lol" in a profile and I think insecure, young, clueless, nervous, or lacking in social skills.

Is that the impression you want to make?

No.

You're better than that.

(At least I hope you are.)

So, show it.

STEP FIVE —
SHOW SOME CONFIDENCE

Let's chat about this whole you being you thing again.

Here's the deal: You're only going to find someone you're compatible with if you're honest about who you are.

Me? I'm looking at everything you put up on that site to get a feel for you. I look at your pictures, what you write about yourself, your personality profile if there is one, and any questions you answer.

One of the sites I've been on asks some crazy shit. You know the one, right?

The one that wants to know if you cross-dress or like golden showers or would be willing to make loud animal noises during sex if your partner asked?

If that's not your deal, it's *okay to say no*.

It's okay to say that not in a million years would you let someone pee on you.

That doesn't make you boring. That just makes you someone who doesn't like to be peed on.

It's fine. Really, it is.

(Women might even like you for that. I certainly would.)

Own who you are.

Look, the "cool kids" don't know what the fuck they're doing half the time. Stop trying to be one of them and find a way to live your life in a way that works for you.

True story time.

Some guy messaged me and he looked all conservative and nervous in his profile. Recently divorced, accountant-type.

Nothing in his answers indicated any sort of kinky inclinations.

But those crazy questions above? He said he'd be open to trying all of them.

Now, nothing wrong with that if it's true. Maybe he was tired of being a conservative person and was willing to try whatever. Cool.

(I wasn't going to go there with him, but you know, whatever.)

Except, that wasn't the case.

I asked him about it, because that's the type of woman I am.

And he said it wasn't really something he had an interest in doing, but he didn't want to rule anything out.

To me, he was just trying to be a pleaser.

In doing so, he lost my respect and interest.

Be who you are.

Nine times out of ten a woman will like you more for being your own person than she will for being some limp noodle that bends at the slightest indication of difference.

A secret (and let's remember the type of woman we're dealing with here—confident, has her shit together, looking for an equal): You don't always have to bend over backwards to make a woman happy.

A woman wants a man who has his own opinions and interests and who occasionally disagrees with her.

That makes him an *equal* not some fawning sycophant with no identifiable personality of his own.

Harsh?

Yes.

But true.

An unwillingness to say who he is and stick to it is one of the worst traits a man can have.

(Being a dick is probably number one. But being spineless is a close second. There's a balance there. It *is* possible to accommodate another person without losing who you are.)

(And it's this willingness to please at all costs that make people think nice guys finish last. They don't lose because they're nice. They lose because they're not their own person.)

A LITTLE DIGRESSION ON COMMUNICATION

Time to remind you that we're talking about women like me and appealing to women like me. If you're eighteen and trying to pick up women online (why you're not doing so in the real world, I don't know), then maybe this advice isn't for you.

Because there's a generational gap here and young women may not write the same way I do.

So, here's the lesson to learn: People communicate in different ways. You want to signal to this woman that you are like her, which means you want to communicate in the same way she does.

I, and women like me, write sentences with capital letters and punctuation. I spell things correctly. I use proper grammar. I do not use "lol."

I'm pretty sure my profile doesn't have any smiley faces in it either (although my e-mails and chats do).

Other women will be different. Other women will use lol and no capitalization and exclamation points everywhere.

So what do you do when you find a woman you like?

You look at how she communicates and mirror her communication style.

(Just like with body language when you're in person, mirroring someone's form of writing will make them feel more compatible with you.)

Ideally, you would create a profile that is true to who you are and then seek out women who match that, so you wouldn't even have to think about this.

But if you can't quite bring yourself to do that (because look at that smile!), then at least try to craft your messages to her in a way that will capture her interest.

(Or, at a minimum, not repel her.)

(And if using "lol" eight million times is your style, then own it. Just know that you're limiting your pool of potential matches.)

STEP SIX —
TIME TO MAKE CONTACT

Wait. Before you send that e-mail, let's have a chat.

You need to understand something before you reach out to this woman. (Who is hopefully *compatible* with you as well as attractive?)

Here's the deal:

You are a random stranger on the Internet.

That's right. You are a potentially crazy, psycho stalker.

I know, I know. *You're* not.

But as far as she knows you could be.

So, dial it back a notch.

Don't assume that just because you saw her picture and immediately started thinking about creative uses for whipped cream or romantic evenings cuddled together by the fire that she thought the same thing when she saw yours.

Yes, this is online dating and you know far more about her than you would if you met her at a bar, but *you don't know her.*

So don't presume to.

When you meet a woman in the real world, do you talk to her about the vacations you'll take together?

Or about meeting your family?

Or long walks on the beach with no one else around?

No? Good.

(You shouldn't. That's creepy shit if you do.)

So, why would you act any different online?

Sure, you've exchanged a ton of e-mails with this woman, but you don't know her and she doesn't know you.

Do not presume sex.

Do not presume intimacy.

Don't talk about how good you are at massages.

(Time enough for her to find out about your magic hands later.)

Don't suggest a first date that is more appropriate for a long-term couple.

(This means no dinner at your place or her place, nothing isolated, and nothing involving your family. I know you just got out of a seven-year relationship and you miss all of that, but this woman is not your ex, so back off and give her a little space.)

Yeah, we're getting a little ahead of ourselves here.

I mean, you haven't even messaged this woman yet and here I am telling you how to handle your first date. But you have to nail this stuff right from the start.

First message to last, you have to know what you're doing.

And I will tell you that many a man falls flat on his face because he's too eager to get to the in-person payoff.

Another true story:

I was exchanging messages with a guy who at first looked pretty promising.

Until he started talking about how he was looking

forward to snuggling up with me under a blanket in his basement and watching movies.

Ew. No. That is not appealing coming from a guy I've never even met.

So, stay calm.

Breathe.

Back off a bit.

This woman is a stranger.

You need to intrigue her enough that she wants to meet you, not drive her away with an over the top need to create an insta-relationship or get laid.

Now, someone who didn't read the first few chapters of this book and is sitting here saying, "But, that's so wrong. Because I had this chick I was messaging and we totally had great chat sex before we ever met. So, you're wrong. Women want sex with complete strangers, too."

"And there are all sorts of articles out there about how women will totally have sex on the first date. It's like the norm now."

May I direct your attention to the *So You Are A Douchebag* chapter?

Those women—the ones who have sex with a guy within hours of meeting him in person for the first time—are not who we're talking about here.

This book is about getting the woman who shuts you down when you ask her for a fun photo before you've ever met.

This is the woman who tried to politely remind you that you're still basically strangers when you suggested Sunday dinner with your extended family for that first date.

You do not know this woman. So stop acting like you do.

Oh, and this book isn't going to go into how to handle dating this woman, but just a quick pointer: When you do meet this woman, remember that it's the first time she's met you.

If you don't think she's the type to go home from a bar with a complete stranger, it's probably safe to assume she isn't going home with you on that first date.

Try to actually listen to what she's saying instead of steering the conversation towards sex every chance you get.

(Trust me, it may seem counterintuitive, but doing so will probably up your chance of eventually sleeping with this woman.)

Okay. So, now you know to dial back the intimacy/sex conversations for a bit.

What else do you need to know before you message her?

KEEP YOUR COOL

Do not let this woman see you sweat.

Have you ever been confronted by a bear in the wilderness?

No? Me neither.

But I do remember what I've read about how to handle a situation like that.

You stand tall, you own your space, you don't make aggressive eye contact, and you bluff the shit out of the situation.

Same rules apply here.

Because if you show a woman like this that you doubt yourself, she will eat you alive.

(Remember, we're not talking about the sweet, accommodating, nice to everyone woman here. We're talking about that other kind of woman. The one who isn't afraid to say "No, thank you" and walk away.)

Let's say this woman is more attractive than you.

And? So what?

Maybe she's better educated.

Again. Who cares?

She might even be more successful than you.

Does it matter? No.

So, she has it all and you're a couch-surfing bum that can't keep a job.

What do you do?

Fake it, buddy. Pretend that it doesn't mean anything.

So what if she's a Fortune 500 CEO and you work at McDonald's?

You're funny and great at Trivial Pursuit.

Who's to say which is more important?

What you do not do under any circumstances is say, "Wow, you're so much smarter than me."

Or, "Gee, I can't believe a woman as attractive as you would date me."

A real one I received once: "Man, I sure hope you at least enjoyed that date a little bit. I sure did."

I hadn't minded the date. I might've even gone out on another one with the guy.

Until I got that e-mail.

And then I realized I was dealing with a guy who'd been insecure about being there.

(And he didn't even know the half of it.)

Quick point: Men will brag on their dating profiles about how successful, educated, and everything else they are. Women won't.

Which means however impressive she seems at first glance, you should probably double that for everything except her appearance.

So, back to the point: Never let her see you doubt your right to be with her.

(This is pretty much true of everything in life, by the

way. Job interviews. Business meetings. Choosing teams at recess…)

If you don't feel it, fake it.

Yes, I know.

You want someone you can be honest with. Someone who can see the true you and still love you.

That will happen. But not yet.

First, you have to show her that you're her equal.

And you are. Believe it.

I'm not saying lie about who you are. I'm saying be confident in who you are.

Do not apologize for being the wonderful, fantastic, unique individual you are.

Look.

We all have doubts and fears.

We all think we're inadequate in some way or another.

But should you show that in your online profile? No.

In your messages? No.

First date? Nope.

Wait until you're in a relationship.

Think of it this way: You're trying to date a tiger. Do you really want it to think that you're a bunny rabbit?

No. No, you do not.

THE MESSAGE: PART I —
SHE'S NOT STUPID

I know it's tempting to craft that perfect message and then just copy and paste it every time you see a promising profile.

DON'T.

This woman's not stupid. And she's not a factory-produced Barbie doll.

Look at her profile and then write something relevant and *personal*.

I know. It takes time.

But you're not a douchebag, right? You're not playing the numbers game?

You're actually looking for a woman who is compatible with you as well as being attractive?

Well, how many women really fit your criteria?

Not that many. (Or at least there shouldn't be.)

Which means you can take a few minutes and write a personalized message.

Why doesn't a copy and paste work?

Because, right from the start, you're telling this woman that you don't see her as an individual.

A man who uses copy and paste is a selfish fuck who's too busy to spend enough time to personalize his message. He just wants someone, anyone.

I know. That's not actually why men do it.

But that's what she thinks. (Or at least what I think.)

Some men are nervous and decide this is the only way to make a good first impression.

They've vetted it with their friends, thought about it for a week or two, and rewritten it ten times until it's perfect.

But, it's not.

When you use copy and paste, you're not being you. You're not interacting with the woman you see in front of you.

It's like meeting a woman at a bar and pulling out index cards with canned phrases on them.

You wouldn't do that would you?

(Please tell me you wouldn't do that.)

Maybe your initial approach is stilted and awkward.

So?

That's fine. If that's you, then that's you.

I know, I know. You're thinking that it's not fine.

Because when you tried to message women without that copy and paste they rejected you.

But what you don't understand is that you're just prolonging the inevitable if you do somehow manage to get in with that first form message.

Because now she wrote you back. And you have to respond.

Shit. What do you do now?

Have a friend write the message for you?

Are they going to read *every* message before you send it?

How long can that last?

Will you ask them to review your twentieth anniversary card, too? (No.)

What if she wants to chat and you have to respond real-time?

You're screwed.

Because you weren't being you.

So, scrap the copy and paste. Read her profile and write something relevant to what she said.

It's not that hard.

And, remember, one of the reasons you want to do this is because you don't want to be confused with the douchebags.

Don't forget what it's like for her.

See, the thing is, your fellow man is making this shit ten times harder for you than it needs to be.

You know how sometimes you compliment a pretty woman on the street and she hardly reacts?

It's because some asswipe before you complimented her on her outfit and when she said, "Thank-you" and smiled at him he followed it up with a disgusting offer about what he'd be more than happy to do to her should she be willing.

She probably blew it off the first time it happened. Maybe even the second. But eventually she got sick of it.

So now she just ignores all men who compliment her in public, because there are more creepy sleazeballs than genuine nice guys out there.

Well, you're dealing with that same issue online.

The guy who messages women indiscriminately and follows any flicker of interest up with an inappropriate comment or request for fun photos is the reason you need to put a little time and effort into this thing.

You need to show her that you're not *that guy*.

THE MESSAGE: PART II —
YOU'RE NOT STUPID EITHER
(I HOPE)

Remember the type of woman we're talking about here. She writes with periods and capital letters. She uses proper grammar. She spells things correctly.

So you need to do so, too.

She may not be perfect in this respect.

But, in general, a woman like this is going to expect you to get the basics right.

You're thinking, what does it matter?

Who really cares about you're vs. your?

It's not like your entire married life is going to involve e-mailing one another.

Fair point.

(But then why choose a medium for meeting someone that highlights your weakness?)

This is why you do it: It shows you care.

(And, if you have a professional job, it shows that maybe

you care about your career, too. Because how can you be an executive or a lawyer and not know basic grammar?)

(I hated grammar in school, but I wanted to succeed in my career, so I learned that shit. If you have a job that involves writing, you should have, too.)

So, what are the basics?

YOU'RE VS. YOUR

These contraction ones are pretty easy.

You're=you are. If you see you're and you can't replace it with you are, then you have the wrong word.

Think, "you're cool" vs. "I want to borrow your car."

IT'S VS. ITS

Same thing. It's=it is or it has. If you can't substitute it is or it has for it's, then you have the wrong word.

Think, "It's hard to do this shit" vs. "Don't let your dog lick its privates in front of your date."

(Yes, that's an icky example, but it'll probably stick with you, won't it?)

WHO'S VS. WHOSE

Yet again. Who's=who is or who has. If you can't substitute it, you've got the wrong one.

Think, "Who's coming to dinner?" vs. "Whose car keys are these?"

TO VS. TOO VS. TWO

Easy one first—two is a number.

(If you can't get that one right...man.)

Now, to vs. too. Too as in also. "Me, too."

To as in, "where are we going to."

(They're different parts of speech, but quite frankly explaining it using parts of speech is about as useful to me as someone telling me a food is a carb instead of a protein. Huh? Whatever. Okay...)

Look, I'm not a grammar expert. Find someone who is. Or read a grammar book.

Getting just these few words right will exponentially increase your odds of success with a woman like this.

A slip here or there isn't going to be an issue.

But repeated failures will.

Plus, getting this right is going to help you in the real world.

Imagine the impression you're making on your boss right now (assuming your boss knows this stuff).

Imagine what your clients think of you.

Learn it.

Or realize that it will limit your opportunities both with online dating and in the real world.

And no SAT words if you can't use them properly!

If they come to you naturally, then fine.

But there is nothing more obvious than the person who throws fancy schmancy words into the mix to try to appear more intelligent.

(Perfect example, go read an internet forum where a discussion has devolved into a petty "I'm right. You're wrong" back and forth. Guaranteed there will be at least one person in there trying to show that they should win the argument because they can use big words.)

I know it's a pain to learn this stuff. But if written communication isn't your thing, then don't use online dating.

Go to a bar. Join a sports team. Join MENSA. (Because, yes, sometimes smart people suck at writing.)

Do something in the real world that involves talking to someone in person.

Let a woman fall for your dreamy eyes and witty jokes instead of letting her judge you for your lack of capitalization and inability to use a period or start a new paragraph.

Play to your strengths.

But if you're going to stick with online dating, then master these basics.

Think of it as the equivalent of learning a hook shot in basketball. Or being able to hit a curve ball in baseball.

Sure, you can play the game without those skills, but you won't make it as far as you would with them.

THE MESSAGE: PART III —
YES, SHE'S PRETTY
NO, YOU DON'T NEED TO TELL HER

Let's make a bold assumption here. You only want to date women that you're attracted to. Let's also assume that the women you reach out to know this.

(And let's remember that the type of woman we're talking about here is not the needy type that finds her worth through external validation. This advice does not apply to those types. Those types need compliments *all the time*.)

So, you find her attractive and she's pretty sure you find her attractive because you messaged her.

Back off the compliments.

I know. That's weird and counterintuitive, especially in our culture that values looks so highly.

But we're talking about a woman who has more going on than just her looks.

And, quite frankly, she's probably a little sick and tired

at this point of men focusing on how pretty she is and missing everything else about her.

So don't be one of those guys.

Show her that you're different. Show her that you can see the whole package.

Let's go back to the bar analogy.

You're the online equivalent of the guy who chats her up on her way to the bathroom.

She's on a dating site, so she's open to being approached. But which approach do you think is more successful: "Hey, hottie, nice legs" or "Hey, I see that you went to Duke. So did I. What year?"

We've already established that she's not looking for a one-nighter, right? So….

She's going to prefer the guy that wants to make a real connection with her.

Be that guy.

You're playing the slow game. You can take your time.

It's not that women don't like to be complimented. Just limit it early on.

You can tell her she looks beautiful when you meet for your date, but right now you need to make a connection first. Show her that you can see past her appearance.

I can't emphasize this enough.

Let's say you're really struggling with this one.

You really want to compliment her. I mean, look at that smile. Can't you just compliment her smile?

Fine.

Here's what you do.

Tell her you really liked that picture of her doing whatever.

And then ask about it.

"I really loved that photo of you water skiing. Where was it taken?"

Or, "I go water skiing at the Reservoir at least every other weekend. Have you ever been?"

Now, some pictures make that hard. My profile picture is a close-up headshot, so there's really nothing to comment on other than my appearance.

In that case, you might, might, be able to get away with a "nice smile." But err on the side of caution.

(And please don't let that be the entire content of your message. Did you read her profile? She gave you so many things to comment on. Pick one.)

Remember who you're dealing with here.

This is a woman who's secure in herself. She appreciates that you find her attractive, but telling her that at the expense of making a genuine connection is not going to earn you any brownie points.

Oh, and for any of you who happen to have picked up certain dating advice books written by men who wear aviator glasses and fur coats in DC in June—this is not that "neg" thing.

We're not talking about insulting her.

This is about doing what most men don't do and looking past the picture to the woman behind the sexy hair and great smile.

Look. There *are* women out there who will soak up every single comment you throw their way and want more.

But not this woman.

You need to be able to tell the difference between the two.

(If you can master that skill and learn to read women well, then you'll actually succeed with both types.)

In my experience, way too many men assume that all women have to be flattered at every turn and that's just not true.

It comes off feeling fake to me. Like I'm with a guy who secretly doesn't believe he should be with me.

I start to wonder what he knows about himself that I don't know. I start to look for his flaws.

Do you compliment your friends all the time? No.

They're your friends. You're equals.

You just hang out with them.

Well, do the same with this woman.

And, broad generalization here, but men tend to give compliments that are looks-based.

When you only comment on a woman's appearance, she's going to start to think that's all you value about her.

And who wants to be with a guy who will leave the minute she gains a few pounds?

Has a health issue?

Or, heaven forbid, gets old?

Valuing someone solely for their appearance will not lead to long-term happiness. Looks fade.

Okay, so it's settled.

You're going to comment on something other than her appearance when you message her.

Great.

Now, and I know *you* won't do this, but I have to say it, just in case.

Please, oh please, oh please, do not refer to her by some sort of looks-oriented name.

What do I mean by this?

No, "Hey, beautiful." Or, "Morning, gorgeous."

You can get away with this once.

But doing so repeatedly? No.

And from the first message? NO.

It says you don't see her as an individual.

Hell, it says you've probably forgotten her name and you just call every woman Baby, Sexy, etc.

Stop it. Stop it right now.

THE MESSAGE: PART IV — WATCH YOUR TIMING

This woman needs to believe that you took more than thirty seconds before you decided to message her.

Remember, you're not the douche who's looking for someone to have chat sex with tonight.

You're looking for something lasting. Which means you have time to develop this.

So, do not, under any circumstances, shoot off a quick message to a woman you see is online right now.

What? Why not?

Let me tell you the female experience of this:

She logs into the site to check her messages, update her profile, or look for great guys like you.

And as she's doing whatever it is she came on this site to do, there's a little pop-up box in the bottom corner that's telling her "Rocketboy 123 is checking you out right now!" followed by "Joe1972 is checking you out right now!" Followed by…

You get the picture? These guys are piling up in the corner of her screen.

(Literally on at least one site I know of.)

And then. Then she starts getting messages. "Hey hawtie! Howzit?"

Do you want to put yourself in there with those guys?

No. No, you do not.

So, if you see that she's online, wait to check out her profile. And wait to message her. Give her space.

(This doesn't happen on every site, but it did on the last one I was on and man was it a nightmare. It made me hesitate to go on there at all. I tried different times of day hoping that maybe that would make a difference. It didn't.)

So, what does happen if you just can't stop yourself?

You see her profile, check her out, and shoot off a quick message hoping to catch her attention.

Now what?

Well, first, you probably didn't follow any of the advice above about finding something in her profile to discuss or complimenting her on something other than her photo.

You sent a one-liner. Or a copy and paste. Because you were rushing.

So now she sees your message.

And she thinks, "Wow. Let me see. I logged on two minutes ago. This guy checked me out a minute ago, and now I have a message from him that says *nothing*. Chances that he looked at anything other than my profile picture? None. Odds this is going to go well? Minimal. He's put it all off on me. Next."

Don't do it. Trust me. No woman is such a hot commodity that she's only going to be on this site for a day.

(And if she does drop off the site after a day it's probably because of the sheer number of guys who did exactly what I'm telling you not to do. Remember, *your fellow man is your worst enemy*.)

THE MESSAGE: PART V — SUMMING IT UP

So, what do you say in that first message?

This is easy. You look at her profile, you see something you have in common or that intrigues you, and you write her a message about it.

"Hey, I'm Bill. Saw in your profile that you like to do underwater basket weaving in your spare time. That's so cool. How'd you get into it?"

You also need to give her something to respond to.

(And should do that in all of your messages to her. Many a guy has lost his way by responding to the last message a woman sent without giving her a way to extend the conversation.)

Ask her a question and she may just respond out of politeness, which gives you another chance to impress her.

Send an e-mail that only answers her questions and you have to hope she's interested enough in you to push the conversation forward.

That's why something like this doesn't really work: "Cool profile. Awesome that you like underwater basket weaving."

If she's nice you'll get a "Thanks."

If she's not, or she's stressed by all the other messages she's receiving, she won't respond at all.

That message doesn't invite her to have a conversation with you. It's just a comment.

To her, it says you're probably not interested, but saw her profile and just wanted to say that one thing.

(Because this woman has a lifetime of experience that tells her that if a man is actually interested in her he'll act like he is.)

Okay. So you send her a personal message and play into her sense of politeness by asking a question that requires a response.

DO NOT ask for a date at this stage.

(Unless her profile says that she'd rather just skip this whole exchanging of messages thing and get right to the awkward coffee date.)

She needs to vet you and make sure you aren't a serial killer or some guy with serious anger issues before she meets you in the real world.

(Again, not every woman thinks this way. Some women are sweet and blissfully naïve about the variety of men in this world and assume that a guy who can afford to be online and chatting with her must be a good upstanding citizen.)

(So not true. Even prisoners get computer access. And even doctors can be abusive fucks.)

(But this book isn't for those women and you're not trying to get one of those women, so let's move along.)

Also, if you're funny it should show in your profile, but now would be a good time to show that sense of humor.

No need to force it, though. Just be you.

So, something simple. Something personal. And something that requires a response.

STEP SEVEN —
WHAT TO DO IF SHE RESPONDS

She responded! That attractive, compatible woman that you'd love to get to know better actually responded to your message.

Oh man, this is for real.

Congratulations!

Now, *keep your cool*.

This is not the time to send her a message gushing about how beautiful her hair is.

Nor is it the time to get all nervous and confess to her that you were worried she'd never respond to you.

This is the time to take a few breaths, step away from the keyboard, and relax.

Go for a run. Go to a movie.

Do not, under any circumstances, try to start a chat conversation with her.

She responded to one message.

You have a long, long way to go.

Pace yourself.

COMMUNICATION: PART I —
LET HER BREATHE

I promise, she won't run away.

She messaged you back, so you know she was interested enough (or stupid enough) to be open to dialogue.

In the same way you don't start kissing some woman's neck just because she let you buy her a drink, you don't start spamming some woman because she responded to your message.

Especially if you have a smartphone.

Do this right now: Delete the dating site app from your phone.

I'm serious.

Unless you're just looking for a casual hook-up, having that app on your phone is going to fuck you up.

Delete it.

Here's what happens if you don't:

You're at the grocery store and you're bored. So you check the site.

Oh, look. The woman you like is online. Or she just messaged you.

Well, you have a few minutes, might as well message her back.

Don't.

There will come a time when this works. It is not now.

(The time when this works is when she's just as eager to communicate with you as you are to communicate with her. You'll feel it when this happens. She'll respond almost instantly to your messages. Until that time, play it cool.)

So, why is responding right away such a bad thing? It's just a little message, right?

Wrong.

What would you think of a woman who calls you too much?

You'd think she's needy, maybe? Desperate?

How quickly does "she seemed attractive" turn into "maybe I should check on the rabbit?"

Or, "Damn. I can never go back to my favorite bar because she's there all the time."

So, what do you think a woman is going to think of you if you respond within minutes of her messaging you.

Needy. Desperate. Is he really employed? Does he have anything else going on in his life?

Back away. Limit it to once a day.

Don't wait two weeks or you'll lose her, but don't jump all over her every single time she shows any sign of a positive response.

If you think you've reached that stage where she wants to hear from you more often, now is the time to listen to what she says when she responds.

I tend to give a warning before I drop someone for this because we are in a different day and age and some people have no issue with insta-communication.

So, I might try something non-verbal first.

If a guy responds within five minutes of my last message, I might wait two days to respond. I'm telling him with my actions that he's losing my interest.

(No, I don't sit there and calculate how long I'll make him wait. It's more of a "Ugh. If I write him back right now, he's just going to write me again. Maybe I'll get back to him tomorrow.")

If that doesn't work, I usually say something.

Like, "Wow! You certainly respond quickly. Not going to get fired for always being on your cell phone are you?"

Yes, it is a bit passive-aggressive.

Yes, I could just come out and say, "Dude. Give it a rest, would you?"

But I try subtlety first.

I had one guy who was like this.

I tried to respond at different times of day.

I asked if he had a job since he always responded immediately.

Finally, I just quit responding.

But he followed up.

"Hey, beautiful, haven't heard from you in a few days." (Note: Don't do the beautiful thing…)

I was in a mellow stage and decided to give him another shot.

(See, even I let men get away with these things every once in a while.)

So, I said something like, "Yeah, sorry 'bout that. You wore me out responding to my messages so quickly. Gotta give a girl a little breathing room, you know?"

And what did he do?

Wrote me back in about two minutes.

Do you think I ever responded to him again?

Nope.

Don't do what that guy did.

Listen to what a woman is trying to tell you. Pay attention to how she reacts to what you say.

Give her the space she needs to like you.

Some other guy is not going to steal her from you.

(And if he does, then maybe she wasn't the one for you anyway?)

COMMUNICATION: PART II — LISTEN

We already touched on this before, but let's touch on it again.

The key to success with any woman is to listen to what she's telling you. Verbal and non-verbal.

Sure, there are some general pointers that will help you be more successful with all women.

But, the key to getting *this* particular woman to take an interest in you is to figure out what *she* wants.

Women are not interchangeable. They are not one size fits all.

They don't all value money and prestige. They don't all care about fashion.

You need to figure out what this woman is looking for and tell her how you can provide that.

(No, not in some cheesy job-interview/sales-presentation way.)

But if a woman shows on her profile that she likes to be active and spend time outdoors (by, I don't know mentioning active, outdoorsy hobbies or posting outdoorsy photos) then you talk about how you, too, like to be active and spend time outdoors.

If she's a voracious reader, then you talk to her about books.

If it's true, that is.

(True story. I knew a guy who spent six months grooming a woman he wanted to date because he'd heard how hard to get she was and liked the challenge. He created an entirely false persona to win her—down to the books he liked and classes he took.)

(He succeeded. But that man was a sociopath with no respect for anyone else's feelings. You are not. Don't act like one.)

You also need to figure out what a woman likes or doesn't like when it comes to romantic gestures, because if you get it wrong—too much or too little—you may very well lose your chance.

I was on a site that let you send virtual gifts to people. I found them cheesy and stupid, so no need for anyone to waste their virtual roses on me.

This one guy would send me a virtual gift with *every single message*.

I would respond with something like, "Thank you for the roses, but really, that's not necessary. I'm not much of a gift person."

And he'd keep right on sending them.

I'm pretty sure I finally told him to stop and he still did it. So I quit responding to him.

Because he wasn't listening to me. And if you can't listen at the beginning of a relationship, you certainly aren't going to listen later on.

Another friend of mine was the exact opposite.

(And probably not the type of woman this book is about, but I provide this example to help you understand that you need to know who you are dealing with.)

Her mother raised her to have certain beliefs. One of those beliefs was that she needed to receive a bouquet of roses from her date for any formal dance she attended.

She'd been dating a guy about three months when he invited her to a formal and showed up without flowers.

What happened? She dumped him the next day even though she was madly in love with him.

It took me a week to convince her to forgive him for not knowing what her expectations were.

(Fortunately, when it came time to propose he'd learned his lesson and asked her how big the ring had to be.)

Some women won't care. Some will.

You're best off finding a woman who aligns with how you like to act.

If you like to give gifts, find a woman who likes to receive them.

If you forget every major holiday, including Valentine's Day (even though it's advertised in every window of every store), then find a woman who doesn't care.

Listen to what this woman is saying about what she wants.

Better yet, ask clarifying questions.

No, this is not the, "can I kiss you on the cheek," "can I kiss you on the lips," "can I place my hand…" type of questions.

(Spare me that crap.)

This is the "what kind of restaurant do you prefer for a first date?" type of question.

Do not assume.

Ask. And listen to the answer.

Once again we find ourselves discussing a set of skills that you can use anywhere in life, not just in dating.

Huh. Funny that.

COMMUNICATION: PART III — FOCUS ON THE MOMENT

All right. So you're messaging back and forth. Now you need to focus on the moment.

What does that mean?

Focus on the moment? Huh?

It means, keep your conversation focused on *this* woman and *this* relationship.

You're single, right?

So what are you doing talking about your ex? Good relationship, bad relationship, it doesn't matter.

Don't talk about it.

If it was a good relationship, you may come off as nostalgic for the past and unable to move forward.

If it was a bad relationship, you're quite likely to come off as bitter or woman-hating. Neither of those are attractive qualities.

(Remember, this is not a woman who goes looking for lost causes in need of an angel to pull them out of the muck. No, she'd very much like for you to be capable of standing on your own two feet, thank you very much.)

So, you have kids. And they matter to you.

Good. Talk about *them*.

Don't talk about how challenging it is to split custody with your ex.

Don't talk about how she's an unstable bitch who you should have never married. Or a whore. Or a money-grubbing....

Get the point?

No?

Let's talk this through.

You think that you're calling one woman a bitch or a whore.

But you're not.

You're telling *this* woman, the one you want to get to know better, the one you hope to date, that when women in your life disappoint you they move from "beautiful" to "bitch."

You're telling her that there's a line somewhere that she might cross that will turn this sweet, affectionate man into someone vile and hateful.

Why would she want to be with someone like that?

If you don't know this, learn it now: There are men out there who *never* call women names like that.

Ever.

Not in the heat of anger. Not when the woman has done terrible things to them.

They never do it.

Understand that what you say about other women matters to the woman you're with.

Even when you say these things because you're trying to flatter her.

Don't Be A Douchebag

I once had a guy say something to me along the lines of "I really like how you're not uptight like most women."

He thought it was flattering.

I thought he was an ass.

Do you think I cared that I was the exception to this man's one-dimensional view of women? Nope.

So keep your conversation current. Avoid the ex talk.

COMMUNICATION: PART IV — FOCUS ON THE MOMENT REDUX

Also try to avoid talking about what caused your prior relationships to end.

Because that may not be relevant to the current situation, but she'll think it is.

This seems obvious, right?

But men do it all the time.

True story: I went on a date once with a guy who spent most of the first date complaining that women were always pressuring him to get serious right away when all he wanted was to date around a bit and take things slow.

Nothing wrong with that.

He wanted to keep it casual. I was twenty-three.

Worked for me.

Except he didn't want to keep it casual. Not with me.

So, when I told him I could date a guy like him, but couldn't see myself marrying a guy like him (he had a nine-year-old kid already) he got all pissy even though he'd just spent an hour and a half telling me that he most definitely didn't want to be serious with anyone.

Or what about telling a woman that you split from your last relationship because your ex was pressuring you to settle down and have kids after dating for five years.

Well, unless you're on a date with a woman who has no interest in getting married or having kids, you've just told her that you are not the guy she's looking for.

Maybe the reason that happened in your last relationship wasn't because you have no interest in kids or settling down.

Maybe it was because your ex would have made a shitty mother.

Well, that's not what you just told this woman.

You told this woman that you're commitment phobic. And will string a woman who wants marriage and kids along.

Stay on message.

Sure, a woman wants to know these things. And she'll ask.

But you can always tell her that your prior relationships aren't relevant to the present one and that you'd like to focus on what you're building with her instead of what you had with some other woman who is now part of your past.

(That might work. Chances are you'll have to say something. But if you do, make sure that you don't convey the wrong story when you do it.)

MAYBE YOU'RE COMING AT THIS WRONG

So, we've covered the basics of finding someone and communicating with them. Follow the above and you probably have a pretty good chance at a date or two.

But maybe that's not what you need.

Maybe you shouldn't even be doing this in the first place.

Two things we need to talk about here:

First, you may not be ready.

Second, she may not be the one.

YOU MAY NOT BE READY

I hate to say this, but a lot of you are kind of broken and hurt after the end of a relationship.

You're bitter.

You don't know what went wrong.

You're full of anger and sadness.

You have no fucking clue how to fix the issues that led to the demise of your last relationship.

And what do your friends tell you?

"Get out there, man."

"Easiest way to get over the last one is to get under the new one."

"Nothing like a hot twenty-year old to make you forget what's-her-name."

They're wrong.

You are full of some negative shit right now. And that negativity is not going to help you find a good relationship.

It's going to either get you a series of unsatisfying encounters where you wonder what's wrong with all women (and that's a dark path to tread) or you're going to end up with someone who likes to heal men like you.

Now, what happens if you end up with a woman who likes broken men and she fixes you?

That relationship ends and you have to start over again.

Or, more likely, she finds ways to sabotage you so she can continue to take care of you.

Co-dependency. It's some nasty shit.

So, before you jump back in, get some help first.

Go to a counselor. Go to a priest.

Let time work its magic.

But don't do this dating thing until you're ready.

And if you need sex in the meantime, can I direct you back to the *So You're a Douchebag* chapter?

(A man who may not be a douche in general often is one right after a bad breakup. He's kind of an emotionally fucked up asshole for a while.)

Save the quality women for when you're finally ready for something real.

So, that's one kind of guy who just isn't ready.

The other type is the guy who says things like, "all women are stupid bitches" or uses that c word to refer to women on a regular basis.

That guy needs to stop dating right now.

He needs to sort his shit when it comes to women. Because he hates them.

And until he can get past that and start to see women as individuals, he is never going to have a satisfying relationship.

How can he love and care for someone if he doesn't see her as his equal?

No man is going to open up enough to be in a real relationship if he thinks all women are just after his money.

Or that they're all manipulative. Or whores.

Or whatever other ridiculous crap certain men spew about women as a blanket group.

And because he can't engage in a relationship the way he should, the relationships he does have are going to reaffirm his negative views.

Turns out that if a man treats a woman like crap it isn't a positive experience for either one of them.

So, if you're that guy, go sort your shit first, okay? For all of us.

This finding love thing is hard enough without people spewing hatred and hurt into the mix.

SHE MAY NOT BE THE ONE

We went through this whole book assuming that you actually want to get this woman.

Why?

Sure, she has a nice smile. And her profile is original and refreshing compared to everyone else's.

So what?

Let's say you're a nice guy. Kind of shy, kind of quiet.

You don't do well in bar settings. You're a little nervous on dates.

You'd never even think of kissing a girl on a first date. Hell, you're still trying to figure out how to move in for the kiss on date six.

What are you thinking trying to date a woman like this? I'm not saying you can't date an attractive woman. Or even a witty one. Or a smart one.

But this woman is not those women.

This woman is snarky.

She's not afraid to say what she thinks and sometimes it isn't very nice.

She's hard to keep up with.

Do you think that profile is an act?

Do you think she's actually all warm and soft and just put up a slightly hostile profile for kicks? No.

(Okay, well, maybe just that once…)

No. Chances are she probably toned down her more negative qualities in that profile.

I've dated guys like that. And it's painful. Do you know how bad it feels to have some guy stutter his way through asking you out and know that there is no chance in hell that it's going to work?

I've tried.

When I was younger, I said yes to a few guys like that. It was a disaster.

It's not a matter of being too nice.

If you're a nice guy, don't lose who you are.

It's that nice guys sometimes try to date women who aren't nice. At least, not in the same way.

I have said it before, I will say it again:

Look past the smile.

Look past the eyes.

And the hair. And the curves.

Read what the woman is saying. *Really* read it.

And ask yourself if that's the kind of woman you want to deal with every single day.

Now maybe you're not the nice guy.

Maybe you're the asshole.

The guy who says, "get over yourself" every time a woman gets angry.

You see that profile and you don't give a shit how snarky the woman is because she's hot and you don't take crap from anyone.

Stop. Walk away.

Because you know what you're about to do?

Where a nice guy tries to pat the fire out with his bare hands and ends up burned, you're going to throw gasoline on the situation and turn it into a wildfire.

Is that how you want to live your life?

Is that the relationship you want to come home to?

Why do that to yourself? Or her?

If you know you're just going to be an ass when this woman's angry, then walk away. Find someone you care enough about to help.

Maybe you're neither of those guys.

She still may not be the one for you.

Ask yourself—what type of woman will make you happy?

Will this woman improve your life?

If yes, then contact her.

If not, then don't

And remember, you cannot tell the type of person from the photo. You can't.

(You can tell a *lot* from a photo, but the wrong parts of your mind are working when you're looking at that photo, so you need to focus on the words first.)

Look at what she's saying.

She's putting her best foot forward (or the best foot forward that she cares to put forward).

If you can already see warning signs, seriously reconsider getting to know this woman better.

There are other women out there. Better women.

I know it doesn't feel like that at times, but there really are.

Don't compromise. It'll make you miserable.

SUMMING IT UP

It's easy with dating (online in particular) to focus on the physical. To see a pretty smile and think you've found the woman for you.

Don't do that.

Looks don't mean everything.

You need to know if you're compatible with this woman first.

And you have a wealth of information available. So use it.

What does this woman want? What does she like?

Maybe what she said is complete bullshit, but it's what she chose to tell you. Pay attention.

And be honest with yourself. Is this really the kind of person you want to be with?

Don't choose someone you'd have to contort yourself to match.

Choose someone you can be yourself with.

And once you've found someone like that, approach her with confidence.

Because, whatever your flaws and limitations, you also

have strengths. And it's those strengths that make you worthy of this woman.

Do it in a way that makes it clear that you're interested in her.

Her. Not just any woman. *This* woman.

Do it in a way that shows her that you're a quality guy. That you like women.

Be her equal.

Remember that you're a complete stranger to this woman, so take it slow and give her the space to like you back.

Do all this and you know what? You'll be ahead of 95% of the guys out there.

(And you may even find yourself doing better at work, too. Because a lot of this shit applies as much to work as to dating.)

POSTSCRIPT: THIS THING CALLED THE REAL WORLD

Online dating isn't for everyone.

There's this thing called the real world where you can go and do the things you love to do and find other people who love to do those same things and form a connection with them.

One of those people might even be a woman that you can date. Or you might meet guys who know women you can date.

It's crazy how that works.

(Happens all the time, though. And should probably happen more.)

Online dating is an easy out.

You can hide behind a keyboard and pretend that you're making progress towards meeting someone when you're not.

And it works for some people. It really does.

But for others it can be a terrible choice.

So, if you've tried it and you're not finding what you're looking for, step away from the computer.

Pursue your passions, whatever they may be.

Do what you love and look for people who love it, too.

Oh, and when you meet someone interesting, stop.

Hold back. Get to know them through the activity.

Don't be that guy who hovers around a woman to get her attention.

Do your thing. Smile occasionally and be friendly, but be confident enough to let something develop.

Trust me. If she's interested, you'll see the signs.

(Hint: If she always seems to be around, you're doing well.)

(Either that or you have a really attractive best friend that she likes.)

Let her signal her interest and *then* you can ask her out. Not before.

Some people are an acquired taste. Give her the time to acquire it.

WHAT IF IT STILL ISN'T ENOUGH?

I let a buddy of mine read this book and he said something about how he'd done all these things and still struck out.

But he hadn't really.

I've known him for ten years and he's had plenty of dates from online dating.

What he didn't find were satisfying relationships.

(He's finally in one now, but it took a long time.)

Whether he'll admit it or not, his main issue was that he focused too much on appearance.

He went through a lot of heartache because he kept looking for women who were 8's or 9's and ignoring their issues.

And he'd stick in there with each one far longer than he should've because he was a decent guy who wanted a real relationship.

Look, the advice in this book is not going to find you love.

But if you follow it, you should at least make it to a first date with that woman who interests you.

And from there? Keep doing the same.

Listen to her. Respect her.

Only continue the relationship if she's improving your life and you're improving hers.

Look past her appearance to who she really is.

Pay attention to what she's telling you and decide whether that's who you want to be with.

It'll happen someday. It will. You just have to keep trying and get out of your own way.

Hopefully this book has given you a few tips on how to do that.

(And, if not, hopefully it's given you a few good laughs.)

Good luck!

ABOUT THE AUTHOR

Cassie Leigh is a bit like that Catholic nun that used to slap your hand with a ruler when you did something wrong. Is she sweet and gentle? No. Is she effective? Yes.

She's a woman who has been there, done that, and has a few opinions to share as a result. And, in her own not so humble opinion, you'd do well to listen to her.

You can reach her at cassieleighauthor@gmail.com

www.ingramcontent.com/pod-product-compliance
Lightning Source LLC
Chambersburg PA
CBHW071240020426
42333CB00015B/1558